Historic Diary

Historic Diary

Tony Trigilio

BlazeVOX [books]
Buffalo, New York

Historic Diary by Tony Trigilio
Copyright © 2011

Published by BlazeVOX [books]

All rights reserved. No part of this book may be reproduced without the publisher's written permission, except for brief quotations in reviews.

Printed in the United States of America

Book design by Geoffrey Gatza
Cover design by Michael Trigilio

First Edition
ISBN: 978-1-60964-012-5
Library of Congress Control Number: 2010906703

BlazeVOX [books]
303 Bedford Ave
Buffalo, NY 14216

Editor@blazevox.org

publisher of weird little books

BlazeVOX [books]

blazevox.org

2 4 6 8 0 9 7 5 3 1

For Liz

Acknowledgments

I am grateful to the editors of the following journals and anthologies in which some of these poems appeared, often in different versions: *absent; Black Clock; Bombay Gin; The City Visible: Chicago Poetry for the New Century; Columbia Poetry Review; Cream City Review; Denver Quarterly; Digerati: 20 Contemporary Poets in the Virtual World; McSweeney's; Mid-American Review; MiPOesias; North American Review; Pebble Lake Review; Seven Corners; VIA: Voices in Italian Americana;* and *Volt.*

Special thanks to Ruth Paine for taking the time to sit with me for an interview, and to Gary Mack and Stephen Fagin of the Sixth Floor Museum, Dallas, for their research assistance. My gratitude to those who read earlier drafts of this book in various forms: Jan Bottiglieri, Diana Hume George, Chris Green, Arielle Greenberg, Shelly Hubman, Larry Janowski, Michael McColly, Michael Trigilio, and David Trinidad. Huge thanks to Geoffrey Gatza for being such a great publisher and editor. Gratitude to the Ragdale Foundation for its support. This book was completed with the help of a Faculty Development Grant from Columbia College Chicago.

I am indebted to research and information in the following publications and broadcasts: Vincent Bugliosi, *Reclaiming History: The Assassination of President John F. Kennedy;* Jim Garrison, *On the Trail of the Assassins;* David E. Kaiser, *The Road to Dallas: The Assassination of John F. Kennedy;* Norman Mailer, *Oswald's Tale: An American Mystery;* Thomas Mallon, *Mrs. Paine's Garage and the Murder of John F. Kennedy;* Jim Marrs, *Crossfire: The Plot that Killed Kennedy;* Priscilla Johnson McMillan, *Marina and Lee;* Joan Mellen, *A Farewell to Justice: Jim Garrison, JFK's Assassination, and the Case that Should Have Changed History;* Oleg M. Nechiporenko, *Passport to Assassination: The Never-Before-Told Story of Lee Harvey Oswald by the KGB Colonel Who Knew Him;* Robert L. Oswald, *Lee: A Portrait of Lee Harvey Oswald by His Brother;* Gerald Posner, *Case Closed: Lee Harvey Oswald and the Assassination of JFK;* David Talbot, *Brothers: The Hidden*

History of the Kennedy Years; Lamar Waldron and Thom Hartmann, *Ultimate Sacrifice: John and Robert Kennedy, the Plan for a Coup in Cuba, and the Murder of JFK;* The Warren Commission's *Report of the President's Commission on the Assassination of President John F. Kennedy,* and its *Hearings Before the President's Commission on the Assassination of President Kennedy* (multiple volumes); "Who Was Lee Harvey Oswald?" (PBS Frontline documentary); and David A. Wrone, *The Zapruder Film: Reframing JFK's Assassination,* and Wrone's edited volume, *The Freedom of Information Act and Political Assassinations, Volume 1.*

Historic Diary

    Dallas 13
A Far Mean Streak of Independence Brought on by Neglect 15

    Crouched at the Walker Estate 17
    I Locked Him in the Bathroom to Stop Him from Seeing Richard Nixon 19
    She Could Keep the Gun Hidden Beneath Her Belly 20
    Oswald in Mexico 24
    My Soviet Folktale 26
    Reading List 27
    The Manchurian Candidate (1962) 28
    What I Missed 31

You Talked America Into Me 33

    Robert Oswald 35
    Arrival in USSR 36
    The Red Flag Rises from the Dome 37
    Diary: May Day, 1960 38
    KGB Chronology, Minsk 40
    Diary: Dread of New Russian Winter 41
    We Like Each Other Right Away 43
    Oswald Translates *The Queen of Spades* Playing Cards with Ella 44
    Baby June 46
    Oswald, to His Father 47
    Marina and Lee 48
    Letter to Senator John Tower from Minsk 50
    Letter to Hilles from Lake Forest 52

Lee was Withdrawn in Almost Any Language 55

    Marguerite Oswald 57
    He Needed a Learner's Permit 59
    Patrolman Marrion Baker 62
    Jean Hill 63
    Jack Davis 64
    Buell Wesley Frazier 66

"Kiss Junie and Rachel for me. I love you. Be sure to buy shoes for June." 68
Closing Argument 71
If Something Happens 74

Diary: "I'm Going to Bust this Case Wide Open" 77

Diary: December 8, 1963 79
Diary: February 13, 1964 80
Diary: March 17, 1964 81
Diary: April 23, 1964 82
Diary: May 8, 1964 83
Diary: June 6, 1964 84
Diary: July 21, 1964 85
Diary: September 19, 1964 86
Diary: March 27, 1965 87
Diary: May 28, 1965 88
Diary: July 23, 1965 89
Diary: September 4, 1965 90
Diary: November 8, 1965 91
Diary: February 14, 1966 93
Diary: August 9, 1966 94
Diary: November 5, 1966 95
Diary: January 3, 1967 96
Diary: February 22, 1967 97
Diary: February 23, 1967 98
Diary: October 16, 1972 99
Diary: June 19, 1975 100
Diary: August 8, 1976 101
Diary: March 29, 1977 102
Diary: May 13, 1977 103
Diary: November 9, 1977 104

In the Archives, Sixth Floor Museum 106

Notes 113

Oswald's "Historic Diary," which commences on October 16, 1959, the date Oswald arrived in Moscow, and other writings he later prepared, have provided the Commission with one source of information about Oswald's activities throughout his stay in the Soviet Union. Even assuming the diary was intended to be a truthful record, it is not an accurate guide to the details of Oswald's activities.

—The Warren Commission Report

Chapter VI is perhaps the most startling, because we do have a literary precedent for it: it is Bloomsday. It follows with startling closeness, which is a tribute to Joyce, but this is far beyond anything in Ulysses. . . . *Bloom in Nightown is of course Ruby's Carousel Club. The two things echo against each other. And it is the Carousel Club which is authentic. I have never read anything—*Ulysses *or anything else—which seems to me as staggering as this account. Partly that one knows it [the assassination] actually happened; impossible to know how one would read it without that knowledge. . . . Oswald seems simpler, more familiar, even tragically familiar. Stephen Daedelus had a great difference; Stephen was actually great. Whereas Oswald needed to be great, absolutely needed to be great, and had no possibility at any time of being so.*

—George Oppen, on reading The Warren Commission Report
(Letter to Linda and Alex Mourelatos, September 30, 1964)

Historic Diary

Dallas

I've seen too many 1963 pictures of the Book Depository with that Hertz billboard and clock squinting from the rooftop: "Hertz Rent-a-Car. 12:30. Chevrolets."

It's probably unsafe *not* to drive in Dallas, especially in August. I feel self-conscious walking everywhere I go in this city.

Humidity squeezes into my pockets, the air between buildings sags like wet cardboard. I gurgled on the walk back to my hotel from Dealey Plaza today.

I brought my feeble snapshot camera to Dallas instead of the 35mm, since the pictures were just for reference. I switched into close-up mode by mistake for a roll of film—about 10 exterior shots of the Book Depository that really are close-ups of an inconsequential 3rd-floor window.

My Uncle Richard in San Antonio, who's just baffled I'm writing about Lee Harvey Oswald, was carjacked in his driveway yesterday. Michael, my cousin, called to tell me—imitating Richard's voice in full-bore bellow: "Ahm not givin' you mah keys!"

Who am I to drive a car in Dallas, and why can't I just rent a bicycle instead?

I'll rent a car, drive to Turtle Creek, where Oswald took a shot at General Walker. Then his rooming houses etc., and the Texas Theater, which I'm told is abandoned.

I'm still trundling through the oral histories at the Sixth Floor Archive. Yesterday, I heard Jack Davis, the man whom Oswald sat beside at the Texas Theater, call it "the picture show."

The police swarmed the theater at the beginning of *War Is Hell*, part of a double feature with *Cry of Battle* (which starred James MacArthur, Helen Hayes's son, better known as Danno from *Hawaii Five-O*).

The DART trains are swift little wisecrackers, but the buses slow and prone to traffic jams.

Dallas subway's a little too modern for me. I want screeching wheels on bitchy tracks and the lurch of ancient trolleys.

I can't understand anyone's accent. Michael's ex-wife, Aubra, born in Dallas, says this in the northeast.

"It was my day off, so I decided to go to the picture show. And that's where, well, Oswald sat next to me. At the picture show. Then the police came to get him."

I can't get through a conversation without asking, "Pardon me?" and "Excuse me?" and "I'm sorry, could you repeat that?" I'm sure they're telling me nice, friendly things. All their words sound underwater.

"Ahm not givin' you mah keys!"

I asked my father how Richard was doing. *I hear he gets around a little better these days.* After his carjacking, Dad. *He got tested?* What? *Are you saying he's got what?* He was carjacked.

I just want to find out what happened when two kids pulled a knife on him and took his car keys.

A Far Mean Streak of Independence Brought on by Neglect

Crouched at the Walker Estate

I'm no unskilled laborer.
I came to the Soviet Union
to study philosophy.
    Please, let me
show you some Southern manners.
Rich men walk with a drawl
through living rooms
unconscious of their bodies.
Rich men rise to meet them.

      Evacuate
all thoughts, send them
street-level. We have ladders
for that, hidden in the subways.

The temperature at the plant
reached 140 on the ceiling.
That's what triggered
the sprinklers.
    We made ventilators
for attics. They trained me
to be a sheet metal man
if I stuck around.

I paid a stenographer to type
my manuscript. I learned
photo printing.
    To agitate
light. I blew up pictures.
Made leaflets and identification.

    What good is a mound of dry wood,
    logs laid in a circle.

    I'm the one who knows
    how to strike a match.

    My friend, De Mohrenschildt,
    would be proud. This kind
    of talk impresses him.

A living room, cold drinks,
some fluster of politics,
hands waving against something
out the window.

No one's really looking.
I'm in a corner.

I used to think in words,
their accretions, spells,
spelling.

Moths wrestle the fog.

I can't stop my eyes swaying
every time I'm introduced
to someone who wants to talk
politics.
                        Yes, I lived there.
I was a radio checker.
Everyone was a communist.

My father sold insurance.
Is that skilled labor,
at someone's kitchen table,
cups of their coffee,
reaching inside their bodies
like a dog-catcher?
My brother drives a milk truck.
Someone's always renting
my mother money.

Walker's in his study doing his taxes.

Now's the chance.

I Locked Him in the Bathroom to Stop Him from Seeing Richard Nixon

Marina Oswald

This was one time he did what I wanted.
He could break down the door—his strength

against mine. I told him if he wanted to leave
the bathroom, he'd have to walk across

my body. He must promise not to shoot at
other people. He said Nixon's coming and he just

wanted to take a look. But I know how he looks—
after he went to Turtle Creek, and with that rifle,

to kill General Walker. I held the knob, braced
my foot against the wall in the hallway. He was not

going to shoot anyone else—he promised after Walker.
I held on hard but it's a cheap door, the knob shook

in my hand like it was stuck in butter. He could've
opened it with his full strength. I was afraid something

might happen to the baby. He gave his word that
he'd undress, give me his clothes and pistol, and stay

in the bathroom all day. The shoes, too. He sat on
the toilet for three hours. I guess he was reading.

When I allowed him to come out, he brought a book
into the living room and read in his underwear.

He took the gun back from beneath the mattress
where I hid it, returned it to the top shelf in his study,

the closet by our front door. I kept him in the house
all day by persuasion. We never talked about Nixon again.

She Could Keep the Gun Hidden Beneath Her Belly

He took the "Love Field" bus to the park
for target practice.

Translated for Marina so the words
meant literally "field of love."

They moved to New Orleans.
He practiced the whole month of August

outside the screened front porch.
He loved to shoot at leaves.

I am serious. You don't have to kill anybody.

           "In Russia it wasn't good."

I'm joining Fidel's volunteer army.

           "Now America's no good—
           so it's Cuba."

These Cubans fled to the U.S. afraid of their own alphabet.

           "Only a crazy man would think this up."

Fidel Castro needs defenders.

He measured distances with a ruler on the world map
tacked to the wall of the screen porch.

That summer he read science fiction,
A.E. Van Vogt, Fritz Leiber.

In nothing but shorts,
leaning back the stout wooden chair,

going through books
eating thick August air.

The plane will leave from New Orleans
but we'll hijack the transfer flight
from Key West—enough gas for Cuba.

        "Of course I won't help."

I am serious, Marina.

        "You're just a foolish boy."

You finally understand me. I'll buy you a pistol.

        "I can't stand shooting.
        I'd go out of my mind."

The Cubans in Florida are afraid
of losing everything to collectives.

        "If you want to break
        your neck, do it alone."

You will sit at the back of the plane.

        "I've never held a pistol,
        much less shot anyone."

I'll be up front. Junie stays with you.

Summer, stale bottle, flat beer body.
Sweat cleaning coffee from the machines

at Reily's, sweat flicks down
the sternum, tickles the solar plexus.

As if living in New Orleans without a fan
made you tough as bronze.

As if he fit on top Marina
like a cheap Russian suit jacket.

I need to be stronger
to deal with the passengers.

        "With shoulders like yours,
        exercises couldn't hurt."

Just feel those arms.
And whose baby is that?
I made her.

        "That didn't take much time.
        I spent nine months of my time

        and health on her.
        I made her."

The hot liniment he rubbed on his body
made him squint, the rifle oiled
in his barracks.

    Clip, cartridge, spring—
a gun is the body of a man
etched with a serial number.
He took cold showers,
ran one end of the apartment
to the other,

    jumped over
the living room couch
as if it blocked a cockpit door.

        "Everybody will be scared of me.
        A pregnant woman, her stomach

        sticking way out, a tiny girl
        in one hand, a pistol in the other."

I'll buy you a woman-sized gun. I'll show you how.

I'll be up in the front row.
No one will notice when I go

to the cabin. I'll whip out my gun,

order the pilot to turn around.
I'll open the door and stand
where everyone can see me.

> "Cuba will get along by itself
> without Lee Oswald's help."

The baby watched him from her bedroom.
She jumped on her mattress. He hurdled
the couch. He wanted to play.

> "Junie, our papa is out of his mind."

In September he left for Mexico to get a Cuban visa.

Oswald in Mexico

Last night I dreamed
I had insomnia. That
a woman with "pregnancy
privileges" (Marina?)—
meaning her feet could
go anywhere she wanted—
put her swollen ankle
on my leg.
                    I had
to kick her off. I
had plans. I wandered.

Walked through two
living rooms
till I found the back
door to the alley.
Mother was there,
keeping an eye on
June Lee. I told her
I hang diapers on
the line because Marina's
too tired, pregnant
with Rachel, to get out
of bed. She was proud,
finally, so I got the nerve
to confess. My mother,
my love,
                    I first read
the *Communist Manifesto*
and 1st volume of *Capital*
in 1954 when I was 15.
I have studied 18th-century
philosophers, works
by Lenin, and after 1959
attended numerous
Marxist reading
circles at the factory
where I worked. Some
were compulsory
and others were not.

Marina heard
everything.
She wrote it down.

*There will be no Fidel
in my body.*

I tried to talk them
into giving me a visa
for Cuba in Mexico City,
but the KGB was playing
a volleyball game
that day with the GRU,
like FBI vs. CIA, and
in their tight shorts
and tennis shoes they
tried to get rid of me.
I'd been awake
all night.
I went to a bullfight
my last day there.
It was Sunday.

Inside, the animal
is a street agitator
and radio inspector.
Even the *banderilleros*
must listen to him,

in order to plant
a flag in the bull's body
just far enough
so he gets tired
of his own courage
and goes limp.

My Soviet Folktale

> *After failing to obtain a Cuban visa in Mexico City, Oswald crosses back into the United States at Laredo, Texas.*

All over the headlines in Forth Worth. Famous U.S. Marine defector works at a radio factory in Minsk. In the hospital, violins.

They scrambled the U-2 codes. I joined a hunting club.

German girl, seat in front. Sign up ahead: *Importation of fresh produce into the U.S. without a valid permit is prohibited.*

Marina says you go hunting in Russia, you catch a bottle of vodka. I shot a duck once.

Take the banana from my bag. Spot of yellow in my eye, black-pocked, soft. Sweating cheek against my palm. I'm not a smuggler.

Delicate, the swale of my heart. Neck is wet. The German girl—her hair a handful of hay washed up on white sand.

I wrote: *I think to myself, "How easy to die" and "a sweet death (to violins)." Rimma finds me half-dead (bathtub water a rich red color). Somewhere a violin plays as I watch my life whirl away.*

Night of the violins, a Soviet folktale: a man shoots a duck but comes back with a banana. That's crazy.

Pushed away the drone, the heat inside my head, the temperature of Rimma's face. My undershirt was spicy, wet.

The puffed-up cloud in my sleep—the petty official who tried to send me back to America. *Balding stout,* I wrote. *Tells me, "USSR only great in literature."*

Reading List

I Led Three Lives: Citizen, Communist, Counterspy

The PTA overrun with communists. They steal the mimeograph machine at night and spy on each other after the office workers leave. I'm excited, waiting in the elevator to testify. Lawyers quarrel over me. The wolf's at the door: Ruth Paine confesses to FBI agents that her entire family is tolerant of others' points of view.

Mrs. Paine's Garage and the Murder of John F. Kennedy

"Our President is coming to town," she said in her ridiculous Russian vowels, trying to make them soft as bed linen. Ruth remembers my uninflected "Da"—basically, I said, "Uh, yeah." Marina all fours on the bed as if concentrating, my hand along her back. Marina hung laundry with her as the President was shot on my lunch hour. Ruth would've gone to my funeral, if only she knew Marina needed a translator.

Oswald's Tale: An American Mystery

Rough trade, that's me, because Norman Mailer can't trace all my Dallas addresses before the assassination. I must have lived in the YMCA only when I didn't levitate with some fussy bachelor. If we didn't have a lonely old queen of a gunman who beats his wife, we'd have to invent one to hold off the chaos. It's all very confusing. The next chapter begins with Jack Ruby, wild and snub nosed, greeting high rollers and big tippers at his Carousel Club with a dachshund under each arm.

Passport to Assassination: The Never-Before-Told Story of Lee Harvey Oswald by the KGB Colonel Who Knew Him

This was a cemetery until the Soviets dug up the graves to make a park. I watched frowning old men play chess on Sundays. The sunlight brought the smell of burned toast from the factories. See here, I must have left pieces of my vertebrae behind, like something from Hansel and Gretel, to get me back to Minsk Park. Dragging the last crumb, a pistol in my hand, I say, "This will not end in tragedy for me."

Kafka's *The Trial*

January 22, 1964, the Warren Commission finds out Josef K. had an FBI number, 179, and an annual salary provided by the Bureau, 200 dollars a month from September 1962 through November 22, 1963. The Examiner says, "I am confident the FBI would never admit it. The implications of this are fantastic. I would hope that none of these records are circulated to anybody." The judge's tie is crooked when he passes sentence. With failing eyes, Josef K. sees The Examiner thrust the knife deep into his heart and turn it there twice. "Like a dog," Josef K. says, as if the shame of it must outlive him.

The Manchurian Candidate (1962)

Do you know what we're telling you?
Captain Marco, will you be good enough to lend Raymond your weapon, please?
May I have the bayonet, please?
Tell me, Raymond, have you ever killed anyone?

Captain Marco, will you be good enough to lend Raymond your weapon, please?
A two-piece Soviet sniper's rifle, in a special bag, is that absolutely clear?
Tell me, Raymond, have you ever killed anyone?
Why do you always look as if your head's just about to come to a point?

A two-piece Soviet sniper's rifle, in a special bag, is that absolutely clear?
You will have absolutely clear, protected shooting, do you understand?
Why do you always look as if your head's just about to come to a point?
What are you doing? What the hell are you doing? What's the matter with you?

You will have absolutely clear, protected shooting, do you understand?
Raymond, why don't you pass the time by playing a little solitaire?
What the hell are you doing? What's the matter with you?
How did the old ladies turn into Russians?

Raymond, why don't you pass the time by playing a little solitaire?
What were you doing there?
How did the old ladies turn into Russians?
You didn't take out an enemy company or anything like that, did you, Raymond?

What were you doing there?
Have any other ex-members of your patrol had similar dreams?
You didn't take out an enemy company or anything like that, did you, Raymond?
Notice how he is always drawn to authority?

Have any other ex-members of your patrol had similar dreams?
Raymond, I'm your mother—how can you talk to me this way?
Notice how he is always drawn to authority?
Do you realize, comrade, the implications of the weapon at your disposal?

Raymond, I'm your mother—how can you talk to me this way?
Can you see the red queen?
Do you realize, comrade, the implications of the weapon at your disposal?
Raymond, do you remember murdering Mavole and Lembeck?

Can you see the red queen?
Where are you, Raymond?
Raymond, do you remember murdering Mavole and Lembeck?
Fifty-two red queens and me are telling you—do you know what we're telling you?

Where are you, Raymond?
They can make me do anything, Ben, can't they?
Fifty-two red queens and me are telling you—do you know what we're telling you?
Ben, you don't blame me for hating my mother, do you?

"The Queen of Diamonds"? What did she mean, "The Queen of Diamonds"?
May I have the bayonet, please?
Have you ever killed anyone?
Do you know what we're telling you?

§

What I Missed

The Le Bon Temps Roule Bar and Sandwich Shop—one of Oswald's hangouts, two blocks from Magazine Street—looted after Katrina.

Someone stole a plaque at the bar that said, *Lee Harvey Oswald Sat Here.* But assassination researchers can't agree if Oswald even liked beer.

Shelly and I planned a New Orleans trip that summer to visit Oswald's old haunts.

The intersection of Camp and Lafayette, where his one-man Fair Play for Cuba Committee shared a building with ex-FBI agent and CIA operative (and Cuban gun smuggler) Guy Banister, who ran a detective agency there.

Reily Coffee Company, where Oswald kept the machines greased.

The Magazine Street apartment he shared with Marina, where he read science fiction novels the summer of '63 in the front screened porch, tacked a map of the world to the wall, and planned to hijack a plane to Cuba. He asked Marina to hide the gun under her pregnant belly.

A few mouse clicks from buying plane tickets for last weekend in August. Would've been the weekend Katrina made landfall.

The last minute, we used the money for a car repair.

My letter to Rick, who asked what I was writing about: *I know a bar near Boston City Hall where Pope John Paul II's photo sits next to JFK's above the taps. Hierarchies and mystic wood, I'm serious, the tall pine forest of the mind. One slant of sunlight reaching down to take you away from the terrifying chaos of a jar someone left behind in Tennessee.*

We visited Rick in New York on the 30th anniversary of the assassination. I recall it as "the 30th anniversary weekend," but I imagine him saying: "I remember Tony and Shelly took the bus from Boston the year I moved to NY with Missy, and at a bar that weekend, whatever, he kept talking about the JFK assassination."

The three of us with Alex, a bar in Sheridan Square. We made fun of Arlen Specter. It kills me I don't remember the jokes now, but I do know this was the same year a punk band called Single Bullet Theory came out of D.C.

Someone played "Don't Fear the Reaper" on the jukebox.

Rick and I tried to remember what Richard Hugo said about poems and birds. Alex put his finger in the air to stop me because he thinks I talk too much.

Hugo's monster was desolate and kind, Rick said.

Poems are birds we loved who moved on and remain.

Clinton was on TV saying he's "convinced" Oswald was the lone gunslinger in Dealey Plaza. Then a cut to Connie Chung.

Twenty seconds CBS video of tourists taking photographs of a granite plaque, where Oswald is called the "alleged" shooter for the official historical record, and 10 seconds of the museum Dallas built out of the sixth floor of the old Book Depository.

One of the exhibits, the actual window from which the gunman fired.

I called Rick last summer on my cell phone and left a message, "I'm on the Grassy Knoll as I speak—I saw the sniper's nest this morning—the window trim was pink."

I left out the oil-stained creaky wood floors, dank schoolbook boxes, warehouse humidity, burly ghosts, and armpit sweat.

Tall, skinny man, sober in bleach-blue suit and tie, like a civil engineer just out of college, leaned toward the sixth-floor window where shots were fired, scratching his chin. Connie Chung voiceover: "The famous sixth-floor window."

The window. He chose not to take the easy shot as the limo crawled down Houston. He pulled the trigger with his vision obscured by a live-oak tree.

Yoko installs a wooden cross in a gallery.

In front of the cross, a bucket of nails. Next to the nails, a hammer.

You Talked America Into Me

<u>October 21, 1959 (morning)</u>: Meeting with single official. Balding, stout, black suit, fairly good English, asks what do I want? I say Soviet citizenship. He asks why. I give vague answers about "Great Soviet Union." He tells me, "USSR only great in literature." Wants me to go back home. I am stunned. I reiterate. He says he shall check and let me know whether my visa will be extended (it expires today).

Robert Oswald

A taxicab braked next to me.
At that time, you knew reporters

by their short-sleeve shirts, loose
ties. He held a sheet of paper torn

from the A.P. wire machine,
the *Dallas Fort-Worth News*, saying

Lee Harvey Oswald was defecting
in Moscow. I couldn't believe it.

I built myself a bustling milk route
in Fort Worth. My truck was cold,

refrigerated deliveries pretty new
back then. Blunt steel and glass,

clean but nothing fancy. All I could
think of, this hometown boy,

my own brother, wearing those big
fur hats like you saw in pictures

of Communists. I'd get used to reporters,
but then I was just out of the service,

with a family, lucky for my route.
Your kids never should feel like

a burden. Mother set up
a conference call the next week

from *The Fort Worth Press* offices,
and we tried to reach him in Moscow.

It took awhile to connect, you know
overseas long distance was different

in those days. But we got through—
the Metropole Hotel. Once he heard

her voice, he left the phone dangling
and walked away. She was so much

like Lee, wanted to be somebody.

Arrival in USSR

The train from Helsinki. Discharge papers. A gift from Rimma
      at the Lenin-Stalin Tomb—*Idiot* by Dostoevsky. Stitches removed
in the hospital. Only after prolonged (2 hours) observation of other
      patients, he realized it was the Insanity Ward, dogs barrel-rolling
in the smell of rabbit-grass, Rimma by his side as interpreter. Told the doctors
      he couldn't eat the kasha. It was dry as gravel. Hospital water tasted
wrung from moldy rags. To complain is a good sign, they told Rimma.
      Later, they left. He was alone with Rimma (among the mentally ill).
She encouraged and scolded him. The Soviets come at nightfall, everyone
      looks at you a certain way. Mother's hot breath on his backside.
Not this time—the balding, stout *apparatchik* tried to send him back
      to America five days ago. Not this time, the petty officials.
Back in the bathtub, sticking himself. They know the world opened
      in afterglow on the train, blood smear in the sky.
Believe in omens. Shirt collar soaked when he woke up. Fire in the head.

The Red Flag Rises from the Dome

Dry kindling far from shore. Fat pine aching fire. Embassy bundled him for reporters.

Wise diplomats, the surge of tide-pull. Fat pine chafes in the shade.

He answered a few quick questions for Miss Mosby from U.P.I. after refusing an interview. Was surprised by the interest.

> *Oct. 31, 1959: I get a phone call from "Time"*
> *at night, a phone call from the States.*
> *I feel non-depressed because of the attention.*

Conjurers, look them in the eye.

Fat pine resin. Smear pitch burns the skin.

To speak to the press is the first stage of dialectic, a cleft to dig in the tide. History is suspicious of symmetry. Greased by spite.

Hegel makes no sense when everyone is looking at you. You can't think in their language, they'll know what's in your head.

History tastes like ash on the savannah.

> *Nov. 1, 1959: More reporters, 3 phone calls*
> *from brother & mother. Now I feel slightly*
> *exhilarated. Not so lonely.*

Diary: May Day, 1960

American habits,
sleeping in.

Spectacular
military parade,
all the workers.

    I visited
    the Zigers,
    broken-in
    Argentines.

We dance
play around
till 2 in the morning,

chanteuse Anita.
Sunk in the glint,
her slip,
almonds in the ashtray,
the spell of vodka,
my head dropped sideways,
radiator hacking,

her voice
a dignified thing—
the man who stepped
quickly past us
this morning
as if balancing
a plum on his nose
when he heard
my accent.

    Ziger advised me
    in a way
    that comes back,
    to go back,

first voice
of opposition
I understood.

Ziger respects
the world—

says numerous things
and mentions
things numerous
I do not know—
I start to feel
inferior, difficult,
it is true!

KGB Chronology, Minsk

4 September 1960: Oswald saw *The Wind* in Letny movie house.

6 September 1960: Oswald saw *Babetta is Going to War* in Mir movie house.

7 September 1960: Oswald saw *A Partisan's Spark* in Pobeda movie house.

8 September 1960: Oswald saw *Babetta is Going to War* for second time in Mir movie house.

9 September 1960: Oswald saw *The Commander of the Detachment* in Letny movie house.

Diary: Dread of New Russian Winter

I am starting
to reconsider my
desire about staying.

I give vague

answers. For Ernst,
I read Hemingway
into a tape

machine. He asked
me for English-
language recordings so

he could practice
accents. The letters
flicked like bats.

When I said,
"George asked him,"
it came out

petrified as "axed

him." The coming
of fall, dread
of new Russian

winter, growing loneliness
overtook me in
spite of my

conquest of Ella
a girl from
Riga. Splendid golds

and reds of
fall in Belorussia
plums peaches apricots

and cherries abounded.
Rosa and Ella
were jealous of

each other it

brought a warm
feeling to me.

I am waiting

for someone to
ride me, the
locomotive of history,

someone to dress
up my literary
appearance with a

clean scarf for
my black pullover
sweater with bullet

holes in it.

We Like Each Other Right Away

On the dance floor, they dip like swimmers.
The people.
       I perch, the foreigner—distant, unreal,
        a saint looking down
          from the rafters of the Palace of Culture.
They swivel, run away from their own bodies,
catch the light like fireflies.

In the future, houses get bigger,
their men keep themselves alive
       till their children are born.

Nothing rises unless someone gashes the soil.

U2s fly in circles, protecting
milk truck routes in the suburbs
       from the Red Army—

       anyone can put in school books
that tea was dumped in the harbor,
anyone can skim the grass with blab
and call it revolution.

Their shoulders dark, touching
sway, waltz time.

It's obnoxious, the future is a style.

The savior appears as the belly
of an army in the last stage of history,
       seer and seen the same,
       the people go forth
       in the hurry tumble of waves,
become what they behold.
A hawk, bloody wing-print
on the rafters . . .

The girl I tried to meet
when she came into the hall—
her dress, red Chinese brocade,
puff French hairdo á la Brigitte Bardot.
White slippers.
          This is not Ella.
Eyes burnished, an exile's. Lips drowsy.
Tells me her name is Marina.

Oswald Translates *The Queen of Spades* Playing Cards with Ella

The Russian names
for things belong to her.

*I am ready to do anything
for your sake.*

*~~I am ready to be~~ I vow
not only to be your husband,*

*a servant
~~in different indefinitely~~ forever.*

Ella deals a hand.
A gambler is a beggar

for perfect love,

thinks he can pull
the magic card

from its fix
in the limbics.

One card you can't play
by the rules.

*I love you, love you
immeasurably. I cannot imagine*

*life without
you. I am ready right now*

*to ~~make~~ perform
a heroic*

*deed of ~~unknown~~
prowess*

*for your sake.
But do not*

*wish to restrain your
freedom in any way.*

44

*I am ready
to conceal my feelings*

to please you.

The women of Minsk
twirl their skirts—

we are a society
of rich men

who never lose
our heads

but go on
losing.

*I am willing
not only to be*

*your husband—I am
~~saddened by~~ sad with*

*your sadness
and I weep*

*with your tears.
~~How feeling.~~ How remote.*

Ace beats Queen.
She winks at me.

Marina's pregnant
and Ella makes

my stomach hurt.
She can't understand me

because of my accent.

*I am ready right now
to perform a heroic deed*

*of unprecedented prowess
for your sake.*

Baby June

Dice thrown behind a door.
      Lingering, the time comes,
            a presence, snow, there's no taxi.
                  Wedge like glass in the bus.

leave her in care of nurses and leave to go to work
days of cold Russian winter but we feel fine

Constellations, stories in the sky.
      The disappearing world is full
           of them. A mother is a city,
                it foams at the mouth.

we both wanted a boy Marina feels well, baby girl, O.K.

The balcony by lamp light on green table.
      She is stout. The evening crackles.
            Russian custom, they make me
                wait 10 days to see her.

Dear Marina: You and I are completely ready.
What do you need? Can you walk? Is June still red?

Oswald, to His Father

I hit Marina. Can't help it, the way
she holds the baby. When the pacifier falls
on the floor, she cleans it with her mouth—
she can't see the drift of microbes.

The floors are dirty and must be washed
every day. They tell me you sold
insurance, you know what I mean—
if you keep things clean, you don't need

to gamble with a premium, a briefcase,
some rickety box of soul we call
property. I could not tell Mother
about my plans because she could hardly

be expected to understand. Say something,
Father, to give me back the moonlight
from the rafters. When they told me about
you, I was a burst tub gashed with an axe,

sweet beer sloshing. They said you died
two months before I was born.
A safe, virtuous desertion.
I'd spell out what I mean for you

if I could. Let me put it this way.
I'm supposed to believe this world
was made by a father who turned
one son against the other

over slaughtered sheep and a bundle
of hay? No, we've made it here: at night
we watch the Svisloch River from the balcony,
grazing the green banks of Kalinina Street.

It's February in Minsk but I'm so sweaty
I'd like to grab a rocking chair
for a breeze. I feel like an old man.
Marina's eye is black. Junie's crying.

Marina and Lee

From KGB Surveillance, House N4 on Kalinina Street, July–August 1961

1.

I'm not leaving with you. Take the baby, go away.
You talked America into me. I need to hear the sound of Russian.
Go to your America without me. I hope you die on the way.

Why *can't* I cook your dinners? I wash floors every day.
You torture me. No time to make your precious cutlets.
I'm not leaving with you. Take the baby, go away.

Yes, I spread fairy tales that you're running away.
I just *carouse* with my health. God, your brains are ugly—
go to your America without me. I hope you die on the way.

You don't want soup, kasha. Just tasty tidbits every day.
Think they want your pot of gold? You'll burst like a soap bubble.
I'm not leaving with you. Take the baby, go away.

You don't get it. This is home. My motherland.
You can laugh, but you'll cry later. Let's be honest, for once:
I'm not leaving with you. Take the baby, go away,
go to your America without me. I hope you die on the way.

2.

You don't know, I give and give you every opportunity.
When our exit papers came, I'm the one who packed everything.
One minute you say yes, next minute you don't want to leave.

Why can't you make cutlets or put water on for tea?
It's my apartment—I bought us everything. Everything.
You don't know, I give and give you every opportunity.

When we met, there was a lot in you that was indecent.
I kept quiet about your Sasha, didn't say a thing.
You told him yes, yes, yes—you never wanted him to leave.

Of course, you don't understand the concept of property.
You're a village girl who never wanted to do anything.
You don't know, I give and give you every opportunity.

You burst a long time ago—I get no tenderness, nothing.
You'd leave right away if you saw our standard of living,
if you only knew I give and give you every opportunity:
one minute you say yes, next minute you don't want to leave.

Letter to Senator John Tower from Minsk

My name is Lee Harvey Oswald, 22,
of Fort Worth up till October 1959.

The American Embassy in Moscow
is familiar with my case.

Since July 20th 1960,
I have unsuccessfully

applied for a Soviet Exit Visa
to leave this country. The Soviets

refuse to permit me and my
Soviet wife (who applied at the U.S.

Embassy, Moscow, July 8th, 1960
for immigration status to the U.S.A.)

to leave the Soviet Union. I am a citizen
of the United States of America

(passport no. 1733242, 1959)
and I beseech you, Senator Tower, to raise

the question of holding
by the Soviet Union

of a citizen of the U.S.,
against his will and expressed desires.

§

Letter to Hilles from Lake Forest

Arrived last night—dinner and a stumble on the prairie. Same as last year, keeping expectations low. If I write one good poem these next two weeks, I'm a happy boy. Want to organize, really for the first time, the Oswald book. Which right now sits alphabetized in a three-ring binder next to my laptop. This is how it came out my printer, A to Z. Maybe it's the only way to impose order on the assassination—tame it alphabetically. Start with the mysterious autopsy. Why did doctors at Parkland Hospital identify two front entrance wounds, then later that night (in a second autopsy supervised by the Joint Chiefs and Bobby Kennedy) conclude all bullets entered from the rear? You're a little skeptical, but you've only just finished the "A"s and now you're reading about Lee Bowers, the railroad worker stationed in the 14-foot tower directly behind the Grassy Knoll—*Shhh, I haven't reached the "G"s yet*—who saw three unfamiliar cars and two strange men at the picket fence behind the Knoll. And when shots were fired, saw "a flash of light or smoke" coming from behind the fence and who died three years later in a car crash August 9, 1966, just two months after I was born. His last words—he told paramedics he was drugged when he stopped for coffee. (Bowers's wife said, "They told him not to talk"—that mysterious "they" straddling the border between Blake's visionary company and paranoiacs who know how to spell "Illuminati.") Someone asks if Oswald was the lone gunman, but you haven't made it that far yet. You're still trying to make sense of "G"s like Chicago mobster Sam Giancana—who shared the same girlfriend as Kennedy (Judith Campbell) and whose daughter, Antoinette, wrote in a 2005 autobiography that her father ordered the "hit" on JFK—who died frying sausage on my ninth birthday, June 19, 1975, shot in the back of the head and six shots in a circle around the mouth, a warning to snitches. No Zapruder till you've reached the end of the alphabet. Of course, this is where alphabetizing breaks down: I can't have Zapruder appearing only in cameo at the end of the book.

I know this is awful, Rick, the violence—pure products of America gone crazy. It's become something else, moving between their lives and mine, like when I wrote letters to my brother in Vietnam about Mets games he was missing and expected him to write me back. You must be home from your trip now. Tell me all about Denmark. Did you chase fireflies with Hamlet's ghost? Slurp rainwater from a skull on a foggy plain? How's Nancy? I spent two weeks in Oakland with Michael. We rented studio space again and made more hoary ear-splitting music. Then returned just in time for us to make a trip to PA to deal with the family's continued decline. ("Don't worry," my brother said to me of his son, who lives jobless with his pregnant girlfriend at my hazy father's home, "they're going on welfare and looking for an apartment." My father drinks Amaretto to stay oblivious, but has the spunk to eat pastries only during Lent. "That's my sacrifice," he says, "I stop not eating sweets during Lent.") Shelly and I go to Oaxaca in a few weeks—and, yes, our March Costa Rica pictures will be posted soon, once I organize them. Alphabetically, "Costa Rica" comes after Rose Cheramie, a.k.a. Melba Christine Youngblood Marcades, who watched the motorcade from the lounge at East Louisiana State Hospital (where Oswald applied for work that summer) and said, "They're going to get him at the underpass" right before Kennedy was shot at the Triple Underpass, and who was run over by a car, September 4, 1965, around the time I was conceived. Love, Tony.

Lee was Withdrawn in
Almost Any Language

Marguerite Oswald

This is my life and my son's life
going down in history.

At grammar school graduation, I had the honor
of wearing a pink dress instead of a white one.

And sang the song "Little Pink Roses."
I played the piano. We had house parties

in those days and a lot of gatherings—
and it was everything Marguerite.

I also played a ukulele.

∷ ∷ ∷

Lee used to climb the roof with binoculars,
looking at the stars.

He read about astrology and knew about
any animal there was. I don't doubt

he studied the animals—their feeding habits,
sleeping habits, their secrets.

He could converse. At the Bronx Zoo.
That's where they picked him up for truancy.

∷ ∷ ∷

My mother died when I was quite young
and father raised us with housekeepers.

I'm child of one parent, yet I've had a normal
life—a very hard normal life, a combat

all by myself, sir, without much
help from anyone.

∷ ∷ ∷

Lee read history books, too deep for his age.
He couldn't call me at work, except for emerg-

encies (our rule because my work came first).

But at age 9 he did call and said, "Mother,

Queen Elizabeth's baby has been born."
Nine years old! That was important

to him. He liked things of that sort.

He Needed a Learner's Permit

Ruth Paine

I hardly saw him in English
He didn't want me speaking
anything but Russian around her
We used English when I
taught him to drive
      I didn't have the vocabulary
for that and wasn't about to try
"turn right" in Russian

―――――――――――

At one point he wanted control
of the car   I let him against
my better judgment

―――――――――――

We practiced in a shopping center lot
Sundays because everything was closed

My father was an insurance man
we didn't go on the road without
documents   I was mad
at myself for letting Lee do that

―――――――――――

I visited them in New Orleans
     the family fidgeting
in those shrunken rooms
as if making a household
     was a frivolous thing

What she was facing just a month
from the birth of their second child
Lee going off to find work somewhere
     so he said
& Marina with no prenatal care

―――――――――――

I said she should return to Texas
& I knew enough Russian to make
connections at Parkland Hospital
where the baby was born
where Lee and the President died
I said this really was for them

for the family
> They'd get back on their feet
by Christmas we all figured

―――――――――――――――――

I took my kids to the dentist that morning

Marina watched the President on TV

―――――――――――――――――

She was another young mother with little kids
someone to hang diapers with
> fold them too
Lee came the night before
played with June & Chris in the front yard
He helped me bring in the groceries
I said our President was coming
to town & I wished I could get into Dallas
tomorrow for the motorcade
> He had nothing to say about it
> Just a bland "yes" in Russian
a brown bag of produce squished in his arms

―――――――――――――――――

I heard on TV the shots might've come
from the Book Depository
Marina was hanging laundry & I didn't notice
> this came out in her testimony later
she left for the garage to see if the gun was there
She immediately thought of the gun
& was it rolled up in the blanket

―――――――――――――――――

I worried about her a lot after the assassination
She left that Saturday morning & we both
expected she'd be coming back
> I didn't see her again until
the next year when she testified in Washington
she invited me for afternoon tea

―――――――――――――――――

People can't believe an American
in his twenties couldn't drive
> I've heard that crock about him taking
a test-run at one of those Dallas Mercury dealers
> people saying he drove down
Stemmons Freeway like some crazy hog
I saw how he managed in the parking lot

    and, no, he couldn't drive a car
───────────────

Lee was withdrawn in almost any language
He bought *The Worker* & *The Militant*
to figure out what they wanted you to do
"You just read between the lines" he said

Patrolman Marrion Baker

A gust nearly threw me from my cycle.
It blew my wheels, turning on Houston Street.
To stay on course I swerved some 20 feet.
I heard three shots come off from up on high
And I looked straight up, the corner building
In front of me. Pigeons flying around
The roof, away. People fell on the ground.
I threw down my bike, a woman screaming,

"They have shot that man, they have shot that man."
The *bangs!* came from where the pigeons fluttered.
I pushed through the door, my revolver cocked,
Alert. I met the building manager.
We took the stairs by the elevator.
We saw Oswald, up one floor, drinking Coke.

We saw Oswald, up one floor, drinking Coke—
A glimpse, it seemed, walking away from me.
I asked the manager: "Your employee?"
He nodded. I ran where the pigeons broke.
That Oswald didn't change his face one bit—
You'd think he'd flinch, my pistol in his face,
The women crying all over the place.
But he seemed normal. Didn't even twitch.

Tough to believe, in those 90 seconds
After the shots came off, a man could stash
A rifle, run down four flights of stairs, buy
Himself a Coke, stare down a cop. I reckon
No one *should* believe, but he made that dash
Or the real gunman was some other guy.

Jean Hill

She still sees it in her sleep, the shooting.
She says, "Hey, Mr. President, look this way!"
He turns to face her, then a shot rings out.
It's like a filmstrip scanned inside her head:
a puff of smoke, a man behind the fence,
cops returning fire up the grassy hill.

Two Secret Service agents grabbed Hill,
took her to an office near the shooting
where they questioned those who'd been at the fence.
They asked, "Why did you jump out of the way?"
"I heard shots—they hit the President's head,"
she protested. "I just wanted to get out

of the street. His limo could've knocked me out."
The agents said they'd been watching Jean Hill,
which made her think these agents knew ahead
of time today there'd be a shooting.
Maybe they helped the assassins get away—
and they planted the man behind the fence.

The key clue, smoke at the picket fence.
"Keep smiling and keep walking—just get out,"
they said, and she pretty much ran away.
They knew too much about the Grassy Knoll,
these rogue agents who watched her watch the shots
from the fence aimed at the President's head.

She recalled a dog in the car headed
down Elm Street to the gunman at the fence.
Of course, there was no dog at the shooting
and her witness statement was thrown out.
Years later revealed the dog seen by Hill
was a stuffed animal for Jackie on the way

to Dallas. Evidence suppressed this way—
this dog like a phantom inside her head—
discredited her TV interviews. Hill
saw a stuffed dog and smoke at the fence.
In dreams the worst memories come out,
like the night her *Geraldo* show was shot:

she looks away from him, behind the fence
(she replays this sucker in her head): Geraldo's out
at the Knoll, aiming, and she's about to be shot.

Jack Davis

Jack saw *Cry of Battle*, Van Heflin, *War is Hell*
advertised on the Texas Theater marquee
and he figured he'd take in a double feature.
It was an hour after Kennedy was shot.

Under the Texas Theater marquee,
Oswald snuck past the ticket taker
just as news broke that Kennedy was shot.
A suspicious shoe store manager saw him.

Oswald snuck past the ticket taker,
sweating, collar up, cursing his shadow.
A suspicious shoe store manager saw him
and pointed the police to the picture show.

Sweating, collar up, cursing his shadow,
Oswald walked a far mean streak down the aisle.
The shoe salesman pointed police to *War is Hell*,
where nearly all the seats were empty.

Oswald walked a far mean streak to Jack's row,
crossed in front of Jack and sat beside him.
With nearly all the seats empty,
he sat down as if the two of them planned it.

He crossed in front of Jack and sat beside him—
then, strangely, moved two seats away.
Oswald sat down, as if he planned it all along,
a conspirator's rendezvous in the dark.

Moving two seats away was, in Jack's opinion,
a signal—a complicated dance
(a conspirator's rendezvous in the dark).
This was some kind of covert contact.

If this were a signal, a complicated dance,
Jack failed it. Oswald got up again—
to make some kind of covert contact
with the man sitting in the row behind him.

Failing, Oswald got up again,
but the police turned on the house lights.
With *two* men now sitting in the row behind him,
Jack took his popcorn and fled to the lobby.

"Well, it's all over now," Oswald allegedly said,
as the cops shut down the double feature.
They meant to hold the crowd for questioning.
But someone snuck out before *Cry of Battle*.

Buell Wesley Frazier

How could he do it? The man I knew was such a perfectionist.

On the drive into work, I said, "It's overcast, misty today." All you could get out of Lee was about his child or the unborn one.

Lee told me it was curtain rods wrapped up there in the back seat.

After the assassination, he came from the loading dock area and up Houston Street, beside the Book Depository. I thought maybe he went to get himself a sandwich.

At roll call, the only person missing was Lee Oswald. They let us go early. I know this may sound strange, but I was hungry.

I think people would really be amazed at how bland he actually was.

He shot the President on his lunch hour.

I was visiting my stepfather at the hospital on Irving and Pioneer. They arrested me. But no cuffs, as not to embarrass my stepfather.

I don't remember the questions exactly, but they asked them over and over.

Somewhere in somebody's library in the back, when you open a book. Often there's blank pages in the back. The key to who did what and why is all written there.

A fingertip dipped in water. Droplet in your eyeball. Rising tide, tunnel of air—he could look at you like you were a thumb print on a Polaroid.

The children in the neighborhood knew him on sight. People would be amazed at how bland he actually was.

He wasn't a big talker. Would answer you if you asked him something, but it was usually one or two sentences.

Two officers would leave, then two more come in and ask me the same questions.

They had me looking straight ahead into the wall.

That morning, Lee was quiet like always. His face blank. Like junk fished up from the bottom of the sea.

That room could've been on fire and they wouldn't let me go. I couldn't look left or right. Just had to answer them.

After the President was shot, I ate my lunch. I'm not saying it was the moral thing to do, but I was hungry.

"Kiss Junie and Rachel for me. I love you. Be sure to buy shoes for June."

Yes, that's me in the article. I am his daughter.
Obviously, if I wanted to share that,

I would have told everyone a long time ago. My first
boyfriend wanted kids so the blood of my father

would flow through them. His parents wouldn't let me
in the house. I was the daughter of Lee Harvey Oswald

and this would depreciate the value of their home.
Our phones were tapped growing up.

Reporters in our living room every November,
mother lashing like trees in a storm. She'd send us

to our rooms. We grew up dreading Thanksgiving.
She dressed us in church clothes for the supermarket

so we wouldn't look like white trash when
people stared at us. After awhile, you realize

that you have to wear the right things
if you want to stay invisible. Everyone sent us

money after the assassination—mom needed it.
She didn't speak English well. Dirt poor,

terrified the government would deport her.
When she told me who our father was,

in first grade, I cried because she did.
Next day, I stood up in front of the class

and said, "My father shot the President."
I was put in the time-out room when

we studied the presidents and got to Kennedy.
There I plotted my successful run for class president.

It's different for Rachel. She was born in 1963,
so Lee only knew her about a month. I call him

"Lee" because I remember going without
milk, and all the people like Ruth Paine

who took care of us when he looked for work.
He played with me, and the neighbor kids,

the night before. Rachel can't recall these things—
Lee's a ghost to her. He's buried under rubble,

waiting to be dug free. She thinks if she's patient,
he'll walk through the door and she can make him

a saint. She doesn't remember he beat our mother
or that he wasn't a good father or much of a man.

I tell her if she sees Lee come back to life, act like
it's *Night of the Living Dead:* set a Lazy-Boy on fire

and slide it off the front porch. Nail two-by-fours
to the doors and windows, load the shotgun.

Rachel's date for the seventh-grade dance
came over with his parents; the first car

in our driveway was a photography crew from
the *National Enquirer.* When she was in college,

she worked at Texas Chili Parlor, in Austin;
a travel guide found out, and she became

a tourist attraction. A lot of people hated us.
A coworker once said I looked like a young

Marina Oswald, then apologized for insulting me,
associating me with something so morbid.

These things, and Novembers, can be stressful.
The first time I saw Jack Ruby kill him,

I cried. Lee looked so small—skinny
and handcuffed. The tears chucked out of me

from someplace new in my belly, a gust
I'd never felt before, or since. That footage

gets to a point where it's almost unreal—
this movie seems like it has little to do with you

as a person. Still, you know everyone saw him
murdered on television. Rachel and I

feel bad Lee was never able to tell his story.
He tried after the arrest, but everybody discounted it.

I would've liked for him to have his day in court.

Closing Argument

> *All we have in this case are the facts—facts which show that the defendant participated in the conspiracy to kill the President and that the President was subsequently killed in an ambush.*
> —Jim Garrison, in the trial of Clay Shaw

1.

For me, an old-fashioned patriot, it's radical thought.
Clean, reverent, I filed conspiracy charges, sought

each agency's secret files, the classified contours
like objects receding from fog. They procured

him, Oswald, the way pimps attach themselves to runaways.
Took hold of him, not as a citizen but a stowaway.

Clay Shaw, alias Bertrand, mastermind, stately despot
in bed, who loved David Ferrie, the New Orleans pilot

raising cancer cells in mice to kill Fidel without a trace.
Ferrie's role to fly the assassin out of the United States.

Oswald with his right-wing handlers traveling together,
slant-rhyme gang plotting murder in the Bayou swelter.

2.

The Warren Report is a dangerous fairy tale—
its game to fool you. First, the magic bullet, which unveils

nothing except the Commissioners hedged a whole theory
on wisps. Like an elephant, his tail tied to a daisy

hanging from a cliff—it's possible but highly unlikely.

Second, how Oswald's September 1963 trip
to Mexico for a visa is clouded with a mist

as if it happened in the ancient time of the Druids.
Fairy tales can be destructive because they are untrue:

Lee Harvey Oswald's fingerprints not found on the gun;
the standard nitrate tests proved Oswald did not fire one

that day. And it was impossible for Oswald to wipe
incriminating prints, hide the rifle, run down four flights

and buy a Coke before seen, calm, walking the second floor.
This country shouldn't have to trust a handful of nobles

who won't tell you doubts persist on Oswald's communism;
who don't talk about right-wingers who ran around with him.

Those files classified. Like Oswald's FBI number.
Or the stipend they paid him—200 dollars a month.

3.

Every modern coup needs its scapegoat to feed to newsmen.
He's presumed guilty because he's weak. Anyone who questions

his guilt must be mentally unbalanced, irrelevant.
Lurking, wide-eyed, the government is presumed innocent

because of its power. In doubt, the lone-assassin myth
is resurrected, propped in an oak chair by the window,

true as prayer. Undertaker's rouge applied to its cheeks.
The Warren Commission's stated objective, at the least,

was to calm the people's fears about a conspiracy—
an unacceptable approach in a democracy.

Our government has no right to calm our fears,
nor any right, for example, to excite our fears

about Red China, or fluoridation, or birth control.
Even if benevolent, there's no room for thought control.

I do not want calm about the killing of Kennedy.
Calm. Our president shot down in the wide-open street.

Calm functions like an umbrella opened against the sun.
Dallas is burning, no matter the government's reasons

for withholding the facts from the people of this country.
It's time to shake loose the elephant from his daisy.

Facts make up a case. Anything untrue is dangerous.

§

If Something Happens

If something happens to . . . It was 1958 when . . . If something
happens to Richard . . . We drove the Skylark to Granville, TX . . .
If something . . . It couldn't have been 1958 . . . But how come
Tony doesn't visit his cousin Tommy, he lives in Chicago . . .
If something happens . . . It was 1958 when you drove there . . .
Why does Tony want to write about him, I can't figure that out . . .
It wasn't a Skylark, I never owned one . . . This neighborhood
ain't the same . . . I said 1958 . . . You don't know nothin'
about cars . . . Tommy flew C-130 transports for six years . . .
Why does he want to write about that Harry Oswald, anyway,
we'll never know . . . Tony was always too smart for his own good . . .
We drove to Tennessee but you know how Richard's asthma is . . .
This neighborhood's gone to hell, but Arturo built the carport
for me . . . Gina drove from Montgomery, Alabama, to Tennessee . . .
I know you retired in 1967, I keep talking about . . . Arturo's
a nice guy . . . The 1950s, when we lived in Germany . . .
No, we were based in Trinidad then, once a month the government
would fly a plane over with D.D.T. to kill the mosquitos . . .
Does Tony think someone else shot the goddamn Kennedys . . .
You drove to Granville in 1958 . . . Spiders as big as your
hand . . . If something happens to you, Richard . . . We had no more
problems on the base, I don't know about the other people . . .
They drive big tanks into the C-130s . . . They probably had those
mosquitoes, but we were taken care of . . . We flew to Florida
once a week to buy beer for the colonel . . . You mean to tell me
Tony can't write about anything else, come on . . . They paid for
his school, then he gave back six years to the government flying
those big transports . . . Arturo cuts our lawn, too, front and back,
but I need a translator to talk to my own neighbor . . . That's all,
six years, then he got a job for Southwest, flies Chicago to Dallas,
that's his route . . . You got me—how the hell would I know if
it's Love Field . . . I guess I'm selfish that way, so's Richard,
we think he's in our country now he should speak our language . . .
No, it wasn't the 1960s, I was in Trinidad in the 50s, hell,
I retired in 1967 . . . He better learn English soon, I ain't got
many years left . . . If something happens to you . . . Why doesn't
he write about the family instead of that Harry Oswald . . .
Gina drove from Montgomery, Alabama, to Tennessee
just to pick up Angela . . . Same every day, Chicago to Dallas . . .
Gina has three babies, Angela two . . . You owe one year for every
year of school they paid for, that's four years plus I don't know
where the other two come from . . . I don't see why Tony
can't write about the family, we have a lot of stories, you know,
so many from the old country . . . They piled five babies in back
of one of those SUVs, just those two women driving . . . But now

he's got himself a good job . . . If something happened to you, Richard, I'd hire a couple Mexican girls to take care of the place.

Diary: "I'm Going to Bust this Case Wide Open"

Diary: December 8, 1963

Jack Zangetty told friends
the day after Kennedy's
murder: "A man named
Ruby will kill Oswald
tomorrow, and a member
of the Frank Sinatra
family will be kidnapped,
diverting attention from the
assassination." Two weeks later,
Frank Sinatra, Jr., kidnapped.
$240,000 ransom paid: Sinatra
offered a million, but
the kidnappers turned it
down. Sinatra's son released
unharmed two days later.
(Kidnappers demanded Sinatra call
only from pay phones.
He carried a roll
of dimes the whole
time and this became
his lifelong habit.) Zangetty,
who claimed "three other
men, not Oswald, killed
the President," was found
floating in Lake Lugert,
bullet holes in his
chest, December 8, 1963,
already dead two weeks.

Diary: February 13, 1964

Betty Mooney Macdonald, a.k.a.
Nancy Jane Mooney, stripper
for Jack Ruby, alibied
Darrell Wayne Garner in
January 23, 1964 shooting
of Tippit murder witness
Warren Reynolds, who chased
Tippit's killer but said
man wasn't Oswald (then
changed his mind during
Warren Commission testimony after
recovering from gunshot wound
to head).   MacDonald arrested
for disturbing the peace,
fighting with roommate over
another man (her roommate
not charged) and three
hours later found hanged
with her toreador pants
in her Dallas jail
cell, February 13, 1964.

Diary: March 17, 1964

Hank Killam, close friend of John Carter (who
lived at Oswald's 1026 North Beckley rooming house,
last address before the assassination), stocky house painter—

"a big hunk of man," said Killam's wife,
Wanda, cigarette girl at Jack Ruby's Carousel Club.
Hank Killam came home "white as a sheet"

November 22, 1963. Stayed up all night watching
news accounts, later collected clippings on the assassination;
lost his job every time federal agents came

to question him, even after moving to Tampa
(selling cars at brother-in-law's lot). Received a phone
call March 17, 1964, left his house immediately—

later found on sidewalk in front of broken
plate glass window. His jugular cut, Hank Killam
bled to death on the way to the hospital.

Diary: April 23, 1964

The night Ruby killed Oswald,
Bill Hunter, reporter, *Long Beach
Press-Telegram*, drove to Ruby's apartment
with *Dallas Times Herald* reporter
Jim Koethe, three Dallas lawyers,

and George Senator (Ruby's roommate)
to get a photograph of
Ruby for the newspaper. Hunter
was working on the paper's
police beat five months later

and reading a mystery novel,
Stop This Man, seated at
his desk in press room,
Long Beach Public Safety Building,
when Detective Creighton Wiggins, Jr.

burst into the room, fired
his gun. Wiggins later testified
he dropped the gun, then
changed story to "horseplay with
a loaded weapon." Said he

was playing cops and robbers
with his partner, their guns
drawn. Wiggins's .38 slug went
through Hunter's heart, killing him
2 a.m., April 23, 1964,

ten hours after George Senator
testified to the Warren Commission
he didn't remember meeting Hunter,
Koethe, and the Dallas lawyers
that night in Ruby's apartment.

Diary: May 8, 1964

Gary Underhill, former
CIA operative, told
his friend Charlene

Fitzsimmons a small
cadre of rogue
agents killed Kennedy.

The agents, Underhill
said, were members
of the CIA's

Executive Action group,
who secretly overthrew
world leaders unfriendly

to the U.S.
He told Fitzsimmons,
"I know who

they are—that's
the problem—they
know I know."

Dead in his
apartment, ruled suicide,
gunshot left side

of head, pistol
in left hand,
May 8, 1964.

Underhill right-handed.

Diary: June 6, 1964

Guy Banister, private detective
    and retired FBI agent whose
        colleague Jack Martin told friends after

the assassination that Banister
    and David Ferrie were involved
        (Ferrie's role to fly assassin out

of Texas), which triggered
    District Attorney Jim Garrison's investigation,
        leading to the only criminal indictments

in the assassination. One
    week before he died, Banister
        told New Orleans Naval Intelligence Director

Guy Johnson: "If
    I'm dead in a week,
        no matter what the circumstances look

like, it won't be
    from natural causes." Banister dead
        of heart attack, June 6, 1964,

the coroner ruled, but
    former Banister employees Allen Campbell
        and Delphine Robert claimed Banister shot.

Garrison biographer Joan Mellen
    describes the fatal heart attack:
        "There was blood on the walls."

Diary: July 21, 1964

Mary Sherman, New Orleans doctor
who collaborated with David Ferrie

on anti-Castro cancer bioweapon research
and donated money to Cuban

mercenary training camps in Louisiana,
stabbed in heart, arm, leg,

stomach, and her apartment set
on fire, one day before

the Warren Commission came to
New Orleans, July 21, 1964.

Diary: September 19, 1964

Jim Koethe, *Dallas Times Herald*
reporter who entered Ruby's apartment
with *Long Beach Press-Telegram* reporter
Bill Hunter and Ruby lawyer
Tom Howard the night Ruby

killed Oswald, found dead on
his bedroom floor, asphyxiation, broken
neck from blow to the
throat—but Koethe wrapped in
a blanket—September 19, 1964,

five months after Hunter shot
in the heart. Killers took
Koethe's notes for book he
was writing on the assassination.
Police ruled robbery the motive.

Diary: March 27, 1965

Tom Howard, Jack Ruby's first
lawyer, who was in Ruby's
apartment with *Long Beach Press-Telegram*
reporter Bill Hunter and *Dallas
Times Herald* reporter Jim Koethe

the night Ruby killed Oswald:
Howard dead six months after
Koethe (wrapped in blanket) killed
by blow that broke his
neck, and 11 months after

Hunter shot through chest by
Long Beach police officer who
testified gun went off by
mistake in horseplay. Howard dead,
heart attack, March 27, 1965.

Diary: May 28, 1965

In middle of
the night, Maurice
Gatlin, who was

Guy Banister's pilot
and general counsel
to Anti-Communist League

of the Caribbean,
suffered heart attack
then he fell

from sixth floor,
El Panama Hotel,
May 28, 1965.

Diary: July 23, 1965

Harold Russell witnessed Officer Tippit's
shooting, saw the killer escape.
Russell said murderer was not
Oswald, but two months later
changed his mind and signed
statement that he saw Oswald
running from the crime scene.

Russell, crying at a party
in Sulphur, Oklahoma, begged friends
to hide him because he
would be killed. His friends
called police. Russell hit
on head with pistol during
scuffle with officer, dead later
at hospital, cause of death
heart failure, July 23, 1965.

Diary: September 4, 1965

Found unconscious by side of
the road in Eunice, Louisiana,
three days before the assassination,
Rose Cheramie, a.k.a. Melba Christine
Youngblood Marcades, told police she'd
been thrown from a car
by two gangsters working for
Jack Ruby. The mobsters, she
said, and Ruby were plotting
with Cuban exiles: "These Cubans
are crazy. They're going to
Dallas to kill Kennedy in
a few days." She watched JFK's
Dallas motorcade on television, held
at East Louisiana State Hospital,
where Oswald applied for work
that summer. She told everyone
in the television lounge: "They're
going to get him at
the underpass," then he was
shot approaching the Triple Underpass.
Cheramie two years later thrown
out of a car again
by kidnappers, this time near
Big Sandy, Texas, and she
died, run over by a
second driver, September 4, 1965.

Diary: November 8, 1965

New York Journal American gossip columnist
Dorothy Kilgallen's anonymous Dallas Police Department
source snuck her the minute-by-minute dispatch
log from November 22, 1963, which
revealed the first reaction of Chief
Jesse Curry: "Get a man on

top of the overpass and see
what happened up there" (suggesting multiple
assassins). Kilgallen proved Curry lied when
he told reporters he knew right
away the shots came from the
Depository. She discovered Tippit witness Acquilla

Clemons, who said two men attacked
Officer Tippit and later said gunman
was a "short guy and kind
of heavy" and the other tall
and thin in khaki trousers and
white shirt. Dallas Police warned Clemons

not to repeat her story or
"she might get hurt." Kilgallen vowed
to her makeup man on *What's
My Line* TV show that she'd
"crack this case." Confided to another
friend, November 3, 1965: "In five

more days I'm going to bust
this case wide open." Told makeup
man Ruby and Tippit were friends
and that David Ferrie, Oswald's supervisor
as a teenager in the New Orleans
Civil Air Patrol, was involved in the assassination.

Remembering the mysterious deaths of reporters
Bill Hunter and Jim Koethe, she
hid a copy of her interview
notes with a friend, *Journal American*
fashion editor and former JFK lover
Florence Smith, for safekeeping in case

she were murdered. Dressed and sitting
upright in bed, November 8, 1965,
Kilgallen found dead of a drug

overdose, her case notes vanished—Florence Smith, suffering from leukemia, dead two days later (cerebral hemorrhage).

Diary: February 14, 1966

Albert Guy Bogard, car salesman for Downtown Lincoln Mercury in Dallas, rode with a customer named "Lee Oswald" on November 9, 1963. Bogard wrote the name on a business card. Salesman Oran Brown wrote it down, too, in case the customer came back when Bogard not working the showroom.

Bogard and Oswald test-drove a new Mercury Comet 70 miles an hour over Stemmons Freeway, near the assassination site—famous "Stemmons Freeway" sign that blocks camera view in Zapruder's film when first shot strikes Kennedy.

Salesman Eugene M. Wilson told Oswald he couldn't buy the car without large cash down payment or lengthy employment record. Oswald said, "Maybe I'm going to have to go back to Russia to buy a car."

The Warren Commission couldn't find the business card with the name "Oswald" written on it, couldn't find Oran Brown's "Oswald" notation, and found no evidence in Bogard's testimony that Wilson spoke to Oswald.

Although Commission members admitted Oswald could've made the remark about going back to Russia to buy a car, they decided "doubts exist about the accuracy" of testimony given by Bogard, who attached a rubber hose to his exhaust, the other into his car, at Hallsville Cemetery, Louisiana, his shoes and a stack of newspapers with headlines about the assassination piled in trunk, February 14, 1966.

Diary: August 9, 1966

Lee Bowers, railroad worker
      stationed in 14-foot tower directly
            behind the Grassy Knoll, testified he

saw three unfamiliar cars,
      two strange men, and—when
            shots fired—"a flash of light

or smoke" coming from
      behind the Grassy Knoll fence.
            Bowers received death threats after appearing

before the Warren Commission.
      His car left the road
            August 9, 1966, and smashed into

a concrete bridge abutment
      in Midlothian, Texas. Eyewitness said
            Bowers driven off the road by

a black car. Bowers
      told paramedics he was drugged
            when he stopped for coffee in

Midlothian. Four hours later
      he died. His widow said,
            "They told him not to talk."

Diary: November 5, 1966

James Worrell walked down
Houston Street three minutes

after the assassination and
saw a man running

from the Book Depository
toward Houston in dark

sports jacket, light trousers,
not what Oswald wore

to work that day.

Worrell testified he saw
a gun barrel and

stock sticking out from
the Book Depository sixth-

floor window right before
the assassination. He died

in a Dallas motorcycle
accident, November 5, 1966.

Diary: January 3, 1967

Jack Ruby claimed Dallas County Jail doctors injected
him with live cancer cells after his conviction
for Oswald's murder was overturned October 5, 1966

and a new trial ordered. Dallas County Jail
doctors took Ruby to Parkland Hospital (where Kennedy,
Oswald died) for pneumonia December 9, 1966—two

days after new trial site announced (Wichita Falls).
Next day, his diagnosis changed to lung cancer,
25 days later he died, January 3, 1967.

Diary: February 22, 1967

David Ferrie supervised teenaged
      Lee Harvey Oswald in
            New Orleans Civil Air Patrol.

      First to teach him to shoot
rifle with telescopic sight.
      Ferrie owned mice for research
            to develop cancer-cell bioweapon to inject

      Castro, kept a tank in backyard
to convert into submarine
      for attack on Cuba, took
            mail-order Ph.D., Psychology, from Phoenix University

      (Bari, Italy), suffered from alopecia areata
autoimmune skin disease (loss
      of body hair). Instead of
            commercial hairpiece made toupee from mohair

      glued to scalp with plastic cement,
eyebrows drawn with greasepaint.
      Ferrie, according to Jack Martin's
            November 25, 1963 FBI testimony, hypnotized

Oswald into assassinating Kennedy.
      Ferrie died of brain aneurysm,
            New Orleans Metro Crime Commission Director

      said murder, one day after release
from protective custody. One
      week after Jim Garrison's investigation
            leaked to press, February 22, 1967.

Diary: February 23, 1967

Eladio del Valle,
member of Cuban
Democratic Revolutionary Front

with Ferrie, and
sought by Garrison
as Ferrie's accomplice

and CIA handler,
once told General
Fabian Escalante (Castro

spy who infiltrated
Cuban Democratic Revolutionary
Front) that Kennedy

"must be killed

to solve the
Cuban problem." Del
Valle died one

day after Ferrie's
aneurysm. His head
split open by

machete, followed by
gunshot to heart,
February 23, 1967.

Diary: October 16, 1972

Senator Hale Boggs, said J. Edgar Hoover "lied
his eyes out on Oswald, on Ruby, on

their friends, you name it." Boggs the only
Warren Commission member to publicly disagree that Oswald

a lone gunman. FBI stole Boggs's notes and
Warren Commission evidence, including Jack Ruby's telephone records,

from his papers stored at Tulane University Library.

Boggs confided to Jim Garrison that the Commission
met in secret session January 22, 1964, discussing

Oswald's FBI badge number, 179, and wages FBI
paid him ("200 a month from September of

1962 up through the time of the assassination.")
During secret January 22 Warren Commission meeting on

Oswald's alleged FBI service, Boggs said, "I would
hope none of these records are circulated to

anybody." He vanished on a campaign flight from
Anchorage to Juneau, presumed dead October 16, 1972.

Diary: June 19, 1975

Sam Giancana, Chicago Mafia boss
who shared the same girlfriend
as Kennedy (Judith Campbell), led
CIA-Mafia attempts to kill Castro:
Giancana's daughter, Antoinette, wrote
in *JFK and Sam* that
Giancana ordered contract hit on
Kennedy for prosecutions of Mafia.
Giancana once said the CIA
and Mafia are "different sides
of the same coin." He
was ordered to appear before
Church Committee investigation of illegal
CIA and FBI operations. Giancana
murdered frying sausage dinner, one
shot back of the head
and six shots in circle
around the mouth as warning
to snitches, June 19, 1975.

Diary: August 8, 1976

Mobster Johnny Roselli testified
to Church Committee that
he and Giancana plotted
with CIA to murder
Fidel Castro. He said
a CIA hit team
in Cuba turned on
the government and killed
Kennedy.
    Called back by
Church Committee for more
testimony, Roselli was warned
by former Lyndon Johnson
adviser Fred Black that
Mafia boss Santo Trafficante
took contract on Roselli's
life and "the Cubans
were after him." (Trafficante,
on 1978 FBI wiretap
heard by the House
Select Committee on Assassinations,
said: "Now only two
people know who killed
Kennedy and they aren't
talking.")
    Roselli left home
to play golf, vanished
July 30, 1976, found
in chain-wrapped oil drum
off Biscayne Bay, strangled,
stabbed, legs sawed off
squashed into drum with
the rest of his
body, August 8, 1976.

Diary: March 29, 1977

CIA contract worker George de Mohrenschildt, an ex-Nazi collaborator who applied for work with the U.S. Office of Strategic Services, helped Lee and Marina Oswald settle in Texas. De Mohrenschildt was a father figure for Oswald when he returned from the USSR. Oswald, whose own father died two months before he was born, once told de Mohrenschildt, "The trouble with me, I always look for an ideal which probably does not exist."

De Mohrenschildt introduced the Oswalds to Ruth and Michael Paine February 1963. Marina lived with Ruth in Irving at time of the assassination, estranged from Lee who lived and worked in Dallas at the Book Depository.

In 1977, Edward Jay Epstein interviewed de Mohrenschildt in a Palm Beach hotel for his book *Legend: The Secret World of Lee Harvey Oswald*. They took a break for lunch but agreed to meet again at 3:00.

De Mohrenschildt, whose unpublished manuscript *I am a Patsy! I am a Patsy!* argues the Warren Commission was created "to waste taxpayers' money and to distract attention of the American people from the people involved in the assassination of President Kennedy," returned home and found a business card left that morning by Gaeton Fonzi, a House Selected Committee on Assassinations investigator who wanted to ask him questions. De Mohrenschildt, whose manuscript claims "a terrible injustice" was "inflicted" on "supposed assassin" Oswald, shot himself in the mouth that afternoon, died March 29, 1977.

Diary: May 13, 1977

Lou Staples, radio
announcer who
devoted many of

his shows to
the assassination,
told friends he'd

"break the case."
Staples shot
in right temple,

wheat field near
Yukon, Oklahoma,
ruled suicide but

Staples left-handed.
Suicide note
found at home

("I am bored,
bye y'all"),
May 13, 1977.

Diary: November 9, 1977

William Sullivan, FBI's third-ranking official behind J. Edgar Hoover and Clyde Tolson, directed FBI's Division Five, which spread propaganda against U.S. left-wing leaders—said in 1964 memo to Hoover he would "expose" Martin Luther King, Jr., as "a fraud, demagogue and scoundrel" to "take him off his pedestal and to reduce him completely in influence." Sullivan called this plan "a great help to the FBI" and "a fine thing for the country at large."

Scheduled to testify before House Select Committee on Assassinations, Sullivan shot to death by high-powered rifle near his home in New Hampshire by hunter who said he thought Sullivan was a deer.

Hunter charged with misdemeanor, "shooting and killing a human being mistaken for game," November 9, 1977.

Sullivan one of six top FBI officials dead in six-month period in 1977, prior to their House Select Committee testimony. Louis Nicholas (heart attack), Hoover's liaison with Warren Commission—Alan H. Belmont (long illness), special assistant to Hoover who testified before Warren Commission that FBI had no interest in Oswald when he returned from Soviet Union, that Oswald "not known" to be connected to FBI sources in New Orleans—James Cadigan (accidental fall at home), FBI document expert who testified to Warren Commission that the bag Oswald allegedly created to hide his weapon did not contain "any significant markings or scratches or abrasions or anything by which it could be associated with the rifle"—J. M. English (heart attack), former head of FBI Forensic Sciences Laboratory, where Oswald's rifle and pistol were tested—Donald Kaylor (heart attack), FBI fingerprint chemist who examined prints on boxes found on sixth floor Texas School Book Depository, including print later identified belonging to Mac Wallace, convicted murderer and longtime friend of Lyndon Johnson—Wallace not an employee of the Book Depository, had no reason to be in the warehouse November 22, 1963, or to leave a fingerprint on a box of school textbooks—

§

In the Archives, Sixth Floor Museum

1.

After you got out of the Marines, you might be a good gangster. All they did was teach you how to kill.

Oak light, burlap shade. Live-oak, low-hanging. Wilts in the sun.

Whitewash brick. Warehouses are caves, cardboard icicles drip from their ceilings. White brick. Plain black floor planks clacking.

Live-oak, low-hanging out the window.

Inside the sixth floor, a hive of boxes. Scott, Foresman, *The Three Preprimers*, for first-graders. Smell of damp cardboard, worn warehouse ache underfoot. Pink window trim exterior.

> *Through the efforts of some Cuban-exile "gusanos," a street demonstration was attacked and we were officially cautioned by police. The incident robbed me of what support I had, leaving me alone. Nevertheless, thousands of circulars were distributed and many, many pamphlets.*

Daniel Patrick Powers testimony: "He would never be reading any of the shoot-em-up westerns or anything like that. Normally, it would be a good type of literature; and the one that I recall was *Leaves of Grass* by Walt Whitman."

Elm, Main, and Commerce. The triple underpass will be one of the most imposing sights in Dallas. It will be located at the "front door" of Dallas, since it will be the entrance for Highway No. 1 into the city—the most heavily traveled highway in Texas.

Whitman: *A live-oak growing. Without any companion it grew there. I wonder'd how it could utter joyous leaves, standing alone there, without its friend, its lover near—for I knew I could not.*

Jeanne De Mohrenschildt testimony: "He just loves to shoot. He goes in the park and he shoots at leaves and things like that."

> *Jan 13-16, 1960: I meet many young Russian workers my own age. They have varied personalities. All wish to know about me. Even offer to hold a mass meeting so I can speak. I refuse politely.*

This structural triangular arrangement is known locally as the "triple underpass," a civic accomplishment of engineering genius.

Creating a commanding entrance to the city from the west and an impressive exit from the east.

2.

Triple underpass, three roads meet.

Clouds break just before 11 a.m. Clouds break up. Field wet. Ozone. Bread dough waft.

Two kids carry big white banner, "Let's Barry King John."

"We're not representing anybody, just ourselves," they say to a reporter. "His administration has set down all kinds of rules on the equipment that can be on foreign cars."

> *Aug-Sept 1960: I am increasingly aware of the presence, in all things, of Lebizen, the shop party secretary. Fat, fortyish, and jovial on the outside. A no-nonsense party regular.*

Jeanne De Mohrenschildt testimony: "But it didn't strike me too funny, because I personally love skeet shooting. I never kill anything. But I adore to shoot at a target. Target shooting. Yes, that was his amusement, practicing in the park, shooting leaves. That wasn't strange to me, because any time I go to an amusement park I go to the rifles and start shooting. So I didn't find anything strange."

Overpass on triple underpass, the policemen in yellow raincoats.

"Let's Barry King John—Yankee go home and take your Equals with you."

Bubble top car is on hand. No decision yet.

Where three roads meet, an old man driving a cart insists that Oedipus get out of the way. He refuses. A fight and the old man is killed along with his retinue of slaves.

3.

The *Dallas Times Herald* wrote a boilerplate story of the Trade Mart Luncheon that never happened. Kennedy shot on the way to the Trade Mart as lunch was about to be served. You do this as a journalist. You write what you think will happen before it happens.

It's common practice—even Kennedy's speech at the Trade Mart distributed ahead of time.

The yellow sheet of paper wilts between my thumb and finger in the Sixth Floor Archive. The story of what never happened, written ahead of time.

You do this as a journalist, as if it's happening ahead of time.

Eighty beady little eyes looked down on a strange scene in Dallas Friday—the President of the United States had stopped off for lunch at the Trade Mart. It was the first time the Trade Mart's 40 parakeets, East Indian Buntings, Mexican doves, finches and cockatiels had eaten with a president and probably the first time President John Kennedy had eaten with 40 birds flying loose in the room.

4.

That night Mayor Cabell drank a toast to the assassin.

One of the men took the microphone, the Trade Mart still: "Ladies and gentlemen." Someone shut off the water fountains splashing in the wide courtyard of the Mart. Silent except for the twitter and cheep of a bird, one of the parakeets which fly free in the hall.

Oedipus: *You three roads and hidden forest grove, you thicket and defile where three paths meet, you who swallowed down my father's blood from my own hands. Do you remember me, what I did there in front of you and then?*

"There has been a mishap," the man at the microphone said. "The President has been shot. His condition is critical but he is not . . ."

You do this as a journalist all the time.

This is the story of what never happened, written ahead of time.

> *After flying inquisitive passes over the diners, they returned to bridges high above the banquet floor to blink unbelievingly at the sight below. Secret service agents blinked unbelievingly at the menacing birds—perched high above the head table.*

Oracle high from the fumes at Delphi.

The time, 1:30 p.m. Friday. The President killed on his way to lunch at the Dallas Trade Mart. Waiters cleared the tables while tropical birds flew overhead.

5.

Fried chicken bones in the window. Rifle, three expended shells, live one in the chamber, and partially eaten fried chicken. Live-oak low-hanging out the window.

I was afraid of him. What he did to my family—that slit watercolor smile, eyes cast away from the camera. Oswald shook us up in the living room, like when someone talks about sex in front of your parents. Rain in their faces, their umbrella broken in the gale, your parents out of control.

> *The floor is covered with oil used to drain the heat of the metal being worked. You watch your footing. Here, the workers' hands as black as the floor. And seem to be eternally.*

Reporter's notebook: *WBAP sez car wanted in connection with the killing has been stopped in Fort Worth and the occupant taken into custody.*

Reporter's notebook: *Mr. Zabrudd taking film with 8mmm camera. Has whole works on film. Wants to give to police. (He is at Jennifer Juniors Co, RI8-6071).*

"I thought I saw someone in the motorcade in street dress shoot back at the person running up the hill. I would say about six shots rang out and everybody started screaming and falling down."

Down Elm past the County Records Building. Ceiling fans in the windows, fluorescent light at noon. Square lamp fixtures. Dizzy fans. Diamond concrete trim below the windows, some kind of decoration. Office workers looking me in the eye.

> *At the Radio Factory in Minsk, picture of Lenin watched from its place of honor. Physical training at 11-11:10 each morning compulsory for all (shades of H.G. Wells!)*

"I can almost say that I heard four shots in rapid succession. They went right over my head."

Cement rectangular grate coming off second floor facade at Elm and Austin. Pigeons in the window sill, fixing to fly. Watch me flutter across the street.

"The first shot must not have been too solid, because he just slumped. Then on the second shot he seemed to fall back."

Reporter's notebook: *He explained the President did not slump forward as he would have after being shot from the rear.*

"It was definitely a rifle."

Reporter's notebook: *A puff of smoke about 6 or 8 feet above the ground. At 5-foot tall cedar fence—surrounds parking lot west of Book Depository Building. Motorcycle policeman ran up the slope, jumped over the fence.*

Triple underpass, three roads meet.

Elm and Murphy, catch the 433 bus. Soggy wood plank, wet from morning rain, covers hole in sidewalk. Sags like a piece of cardboard.

Oswald on TV burnished the living room. He could make our sycamore bleed.

I slip, nearly miss the bus even though the driver sees me. Bang on the door.

"I have to walk from where I am going most of the time," he said the morning Ruby shot him. "I have no automobile. I have no means of transportation."

Notes

"A Far Mean Streak of Independence Brought on by Neglect":
"Lee Harvey Oswald was born in Oct. 1939 in New Orleans, La., the son of an insurance salesman whose early death left a far mean streak of independence brought on by neglect" (Oswald, author's note to his manuscript, "The Kollective").

"Crouched at the Walker Estate":
"On April 10, 1963, in Dallas, Tex., Maj. Gen. Edwin A. Walker, an active and controversial figure on the American political scene . . . narrowly escaped death when a rifle bullet fired from outside his home passed near his head as he was seated at his desk" (*Warren Commission Report*).

"I Locked Him in the Bathroom to Stop Him From Seeing Richard Nixon":
Thanks to John Thompson, resident of Oswald's former home at 214 W. Neely St., Dallas, for giving me a tour of the apartment in August 2005, including the backyard where the famous "Hunter of Fascists" photograph was taken.

"*The Manchurian Candidate* (1962)":
All lines in the poem are questions taken from the film *The Manchurian Candidate*. After the assassination, Richard Condon, whose novel the film was based on, received a phone call from a reporter asking if he felt responsible for the murder. Rumors have abounded that the film was removed from distribution because of the assassination. (See, too, the 1954 film *Suddenly*, which also starred Frank Sinatra.) But the film was shown on The CBS Thursday Night Movies in September 1965. CBS repeated it that season. It was shown again on NBC, Spring 1974 and Summer 1975. Rights to *The Manchurian Candidate* reverted to Frank Sinatra a few years later, and he allowed it to disappear from distribution. With MGM/UA, Sinatra re-released it in 1988.

"What I Missed":
Adapts lines from Richard Hugo's "Letter to Gale from Ovando."

"Diary: May Day, 1960":
Adapts lines from George Oppen's "Of Being Numerous."

"We Like Each Other Right Away":
Adapts lines from Whitman's "There Was a Child Went Forth."

"Oswald Translates *The Queen of Spades* Playing Cards With Ella":
Inspired by Oswald's English-Russian translation of an aria from Tchaikovsky's *The Queen of Spades* (Warren Commission Exhibit 53, Volume XVI). Italics in the poem are Oswald's words, translated back into English by the FBI. *The Queen of Spades* was Oswald's favorite opera.

"Marina and Lee":
All lines collaged from KGB surveillance transcripts of the Oswalds from July-August 1961. I am indebted to Norman Mailer, *Oswald's Tale: An American Mystery*, for Russian-English translations.

"Letter to Senator John Tower From Minsk":
Warren Commission Exhibit 1058, Volume XXII.

"He Needed a Learner's Permit":
Worried that Marina might be forced to return to the Soviet Union, Ruth Paine offered to let her stay at her home in Irving, Texas, in exchange for Russian language lessons. Marina didn't tell anyone about the Mannlicher-Carcano rifle in the garage. Or the "Hunter of Fascists." Or Walker. "I begin to shake when I have this conversation," Paine explained to me over lunch. "I only do it two or three times max in a year because it costs emotionally to do it. I feel it's appropriate. You didn't twist my arm. But it's emotionally expensive."

"Patrolman Marrion Baker":
Baker, a motorcycle police officer, ran into the Texas School Book Depository within a minute-and-a-half of hearing shots from above. Presidential aide Kenny O'Donnell, riding in the motorcade that day, later affirmed the Warren Commission's account, which hinged on witnesses such as Baker. But in a 1968 conversation with Congressman Tip O'Neill, O'Donnell confessed that he actually believed the shots came from the Grassy Knoll and that he had withheld this version of events to protect the Kennedys from the emotional strain of a larger investigation. "I can't believe it," O'Neill, replied. "I wouldn't have done that in a million years. I would have told the truth."

"Jack Davis":
Oswald sat next to Davis in the Texas Theater minutes before he was captured by police. Some researchers believe that Oswald originally fled to the theater as part of an arranged meeting with co-conspirators who would help him leave the country.

"Buell Wesley Frazier":
Frazier, Oswald's co-worker at the Book Depository, realized it was *Thursday*, and Oswald usually asked for rides to Irving on *Fridays*. Frazier's Warren Commission testimony: "I said, 'Why are you going home today?' And he says, 'I am going home to get some curtain rods. You know, to put in an apartment.' He wanted to hang up some curtains and I said, 'Very well.' And I never thought more about it and I had some invoices in my hands for some orders and I walked on off and started filling the orders."

"'Kiss Junie and Rachel for me. I love you. Be sure to buy shoes for June.'":
Title comes from Oswald's conversation with Marina, Dallas City Jail, November 23, 1963. Source text for June Oswald's language in the poem: Steve Salerno, "Lee Harvey's Oldest—June Oswald," *The New York Times Magazine* (30 April 1995).

"Closing Argument":
Adapts text from Jim Garrison's closing argument in the conspiracy trial of Clay Shaw, the only criminal case to emerge from the Kennedy assassination. Poem also adapts language from Garrison's 15 July 1967 nationally televised rebuttal to NBC's documentary, "The JFK Conspiracy: The Case of Jim Garrison."

"In the Archives, Sixth-Floor Museum":
Adapts: Warren Commission testimony of Daniel Patrick Powers and Jeanne De Mohrenshildt; Oswald's correspondence and diary entries from the U.S. and the U.S.S.R.; unpublished *Dallas Times Herald* advance material written on the speech JFK was scheduled to give at the Dallas Trade Mart the afternoon of November 22; *Dallas Times Herald* reporters' notes taken immediately after the assassination; text from "The Kollective," a long essay on Soviet workers' lives that Oswald wrote in Minsk; and lines from Whitman's "I Saw in Louisiana a Live-Oak Growing."

Tony Trigilio's books include the poetry collection *The Lama's English Lessons* (Three Candles Press) and the critical monograph *Allen Ginsberg's Buddhist Poetics* (Southern Illinois University Press). With Tim Prchal, he co-edited *Visions and Divisions: American Immigration Literature, 1870-1930* (Rutgers University Press). He is a member of the core poetry faculty at Columbia College Chicago, and is a co-founder and co-editor of *Court Green*.

Made in the USA
Charleston, SC
26 March 2011